The 5 Ingredient Kitchen

50 super delicious recipes you've never heard of that are easy to make and require only 5 ingredients or less.

Copyright © Media Partisans 2017
Media Partisans GmbH
Berliner Str. 89
14467 Potsdam
Germany

ISBN: 978-3-00-057781-9

Find us on:

www.scrumdiddlyumptious.com

The Chefs

Gregor

Cristina

Hannes

Oliver

Since launching Scrumdiddlyumptious in 2016, our fun approach to cooking has attracted an ever-growing fanbase. People love our unique recipe ideas that are as easy to make as they are delicious. Our enthusiastic audience checks in regularly to enjoy all the new mouthwatering recipes the Scrumdiddlyumptious team has to offer. This book is our "Best Of" collection and the recipes have one thing in common: they all have only 5 ingredients or less. Tasty food doesn't need to be complicated!

Enjoy!

6

38

80

Starters & Snacks

Meals & More

Sweets & Treats

6

Starters
&
Snacks

Here's how:

1. Wash the potatoes, you can leave the peel on if you prefer. Push a long wooden skewer through each one.

2. Place a knife at an angle and cut into the potato until the knife meets the skewer. Now turn the potato, keeping the knife in place. This forms a spiral that you can carefully pull apart.

3. Put the melted butter into a bowl and add the garlic, herbs, salt and pepper. Mix well and brush onto the potato spirals.

4. Bake for 20 minutes at 375°F.

You'll need

- 4 medium-sized potatoes
- ¼ cup melted butter
- 2 garlic gloves, diced
- 1 tbsp herbs, chopped (e.g. rosemary, oregano)
- 4 wooden skewers

🕐 Preparation Time: 10 min
Cooking Time: 20 min

👥 Servings: 4

tip —

To make them even crispier try frying them instead.

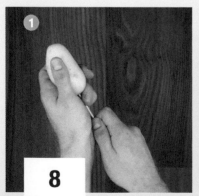

8

Baked Potato Spirals

Here's how:

① Separate the egg white and the yolk. Use a mixer to beat the egg white until it's light and fluffy. Add the parmesan cheese while mixing.

② Spoon the egg white onto a greased baking sheet and bake for 3 minutes at 350°F.

③ Now gently place the yolk in the middle of the "cloud" and bake for another 2 minutes.

④ **Toast the bread, place your "fluffy egg cloud" on it and serve.**

You'll need

- 1 egg
- 2 tbsp grated parmesan cheese
- **1 slice white bread, toasted**

🕐 Preparation Time: 15 min
   Cooking Time: 5 min
👥 Servings: 1

 tip

Sprinkle on some chopped chives to add a savory lining to your cloud.

Here's how:

1. Cut the hot dogs in half and spear each half onto a skewer.

2. Place a knife at an angle and cut into the hot dog until the knife meets the skewer. Turn the skewer while keeping the knife in place. This forms a spiral that you can carefully pull apart.

3. Roll out the pizza dough and cut it into thin strips. Roll each strip to form ropes.

4. Press the rope into the spiral gap of each hot dog. Press the end of the rope firmly to the skewer so that it stays in place.

5. Place your hot dog skewers on a pan lined with parchment paper and bake for 15 minutes at 350°F.

You'll need

- 5 hot dogs
- 1 sheet pizza dough
- 10 skewers

Preparation Time: 10 min
Cooking Time: 15 min
Servings: 10

 tip —————

Have some ketchup and mustard ready for dipping.

  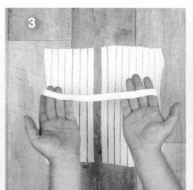 

Tornado Hot Dogs

Here's how:

① Lay the bacon slices on parchment paper to form a weaved mat by first laying six in one direction and then laying six across the top, alternating above and below the other slices.

② Bake the bacon mat for 12 minutes at 355°F. When it's done, use a bowl to help you cut out a circle.

③ Use the two glasses to make a stand and lay the skewers on top of them. You may have to tie the skewers together.

④ Hang the circle of bacon over the skewers and put the whole thing in the microwave. Cook for two minutes at 550W. This will give the bacon its taco shape and should hold when it cools.

⑤ Prepare the scrambled eggs by beating them in a bowl and adding the cheese. Fry the mix in a pan.

⑥ Fill up your bacon taco shells and enjoy.

You'll need

- 12 slices of bacon
- 2 eggs
- 2 oz cheese
- 2 glasses
- 3 skewers

🕐 Preparation Time: 20 min
Cooking Time: 14 min

👥 Servings: 1

tip ——
Garnish your taco with some chopped chives.

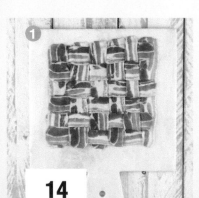

Breakfast Bacon Taco

Here's how:

1. Roll out the pastry and cover it with cream cheese.

2. Sprinkle on the bacon and cheddar.

3. Roll up the pastry and cut it into 12 even portions with a sharp knife.

4. Place the slices on a baking tray, baste them with egg and bake for 15 minutes at 350°F.

You'll need

- 1 roll puff pastry dough
- ½ cup cream cheese
- ¾ cup grated cheddar cheese
- 5 slices of bacon, diced
- 1 egg, beaten

🕐 Preparation Time: 10 min
Cooking Time: 15 min

👥 Servings: 12

tip ———

Add some extra zing with some chopped onions and parsley.

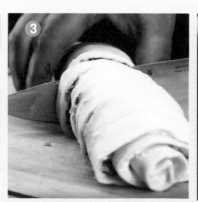

16

Cheese & Bacon Pastry Swirls

Here's how:

1. Roll the pizza dough out and cut it into four equal strips.

2. In the middle of each strip, carefully sprinkle on the diced ham and mozzarella.

3. Press the sides together so that the ham and cheese are sealed in.

4. Form the rolled dough strips into pretzels, brush with beaten egg, and sprinkle with parmesan. Bake at 390°F for 10-13 minutes.

You'll need

- 1 package pizza dough
- 3.5 oz ham, diced
- 1 cup grated mozzarella
- 1 cup grated parmesan
- 1 egg, beaten

🕐 Preparation Time: 15 min
   Cooking Time: 13 min
👥 Servings: 4

tip

With some pizza sauce for dipping they can quickly become Pizza Pretzels.

18

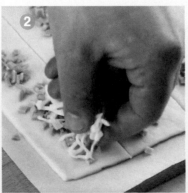

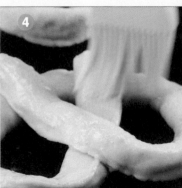

Ham & Cheese Pretzels

Here's how:

① Coat the bottom of a muffin pan with some oil.

② Add a few spinach leaves and some some diced tomato to each mold.

③ Pour the egg whites into each mold and season with salt and pepper.

④ Bake your mini omelets for 15 minutes at 350°F.

You'll need

- 1¼ cups egg white
- 1 tomato, diced
- 3.5 oz fresh spinach leaves

Preparation Time: 10 min
Cooking Time: 15 min

Servings: 6

 tip

Add some crumbled feta cheese for an extra kick of flavor.

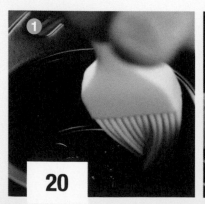

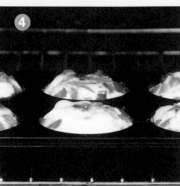

Spinach & Tomato Mini Omelets

Here's how:

1. Cut the top of your bread in a criss-cross pattern. When cutting, make sure not to cut all the way through so that the individual pieces of bread are still attached at the bottom. Slice the loaf in one direction first, then turn it 90° and slice the other way.

2. Place small slices of cheese into the openings.

3. Mix the butter and garlic in a bowl. Season with salt and pepper.

4. Using a knife, add your buttery mixture to the crevices of the bread.

5. Cover with aluminum foil and bake for 10 minutes at 400°F.

6. Remove the foil and bake for a further 5 minutes at 490°F.

You'll need

- 1 large rustic loaf
- 1-2 cloves of garlic, chopped
- ⅓ cup butter, melted
- mozzarella cheese
- cheddar cheese

🕐 Preparation Time: 15 min
Cooking Time: 15 min

👥 Servings: 4-6

tip

Make your loaf extra zesty by adding some chopped spring onions to the mix.

Cheesy Garlic Loaf

Here's how:

① Cut the zucchini into slices. The thinner the slices, the crunchier the final result will be.

② Soak the zucchini slices in milk. It should take 10-15 minutes for them to absorb most of the milk.

③ Mix the rest of the ingredients. No need to be precise about the measurements.

④ Roll both sides of each slice in the breadcrumbs and cheese mixture.

⑤ Place the breaded slices on an oven rack.

⑥ Bake at 400°F for about 20-25 minutes or until they turn golden brown.

You'll need

- 1 zucchini
- milk
- 1¼ cups breadcrumbs
- ⅔ cup grated parmesan cheese
- 1 tsp garlic powder

🕐 Preparation Time: 15 min
Cooking Time: 25 min

👥 Servings: 1

tip

Mix up some sour cream and chives as a tasty dip.

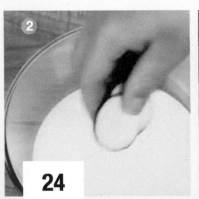

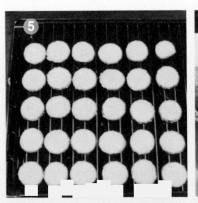

Crunchy Zucchini Chips

Here's how:

1. Wash the mushrooms, remove the stems, and hollow them out.

2. Mix the garlic with some butter and brush it onto the caps of the mushrooms. Add salt and pepper to taste.

3. Turn the caps and fill them with a thick slice of mozzarella and a few slices of tomato.

4. Bake for 20 minutes at 350°F.

You'll need

- 6 large mushrooms
- 2 garlic cloves, chopped
- 2 balls fresh mozzarella, sliced
- ⅔ cup cherry tomatoes, sliced

🕐 Preparation Time: 10 min
Cooking Time: 20 min

👥 Servings: 6

tip

Sprinkle on freshly chopped basil and a dash of balsamic vinegar for the crowning touch.

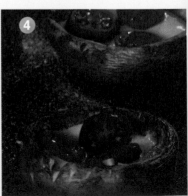

Caprese Mushrooms

Here's how:

① Cut the eggplant into thick slices and lay them on a baking sheet.

② Sprinkle 1 tsp of salt over the slices and wait about 30 minutes. The salt will dissolve. Dab the slices dry with a paper towel.

③ Coat the slices with some vegetable oil and season with salt and pepper.

④ Bake the eggplant slices at 350°F for 25 minutes.

⑤ After baking, add a generous dollop of the tomato sauce to each slice of eggplant.

⑥ Add the mozzarella balls to the top of the slices and bake them for another 5 minutes at 350°F.

⑦ Garnish the slices with finely chopped basil leaves.

You'll need

- 1 eggplant
- 1½ cups tomato sauce
- 8 oz mini mozzarella balls
- 10 basil leaves, chopped

Preparation Time: 15 min
Cooking Time: 30 min

Servings: 4

tip

Sprinkle on some grated parmesan as the finishing touch.

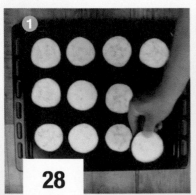

Eggplant Pizza Bites

Here's how:

1 Cut the avocado in half and remove the seed. Widen the hole in the center so that it's large enough to snugly fit the egg. Carefully remove the rind from the avocado with a spoon.

2 The egg should be poached. The best method is to spread a sheet of cling wrap over a small bowl and crack the egg onto it being careful not to break the yolk. Draw the cling wrap together and close it with a twist-tie or a bag clip. Cook the cling wrap baggie in boiling water for 5 minutes. You should end up with a shape that perfectly fits the avocado.

3 Carefully remove the egg from the cling wrap and place it in one half of the avocado, then cover it with the other half.

4 Wrap the two halves together with slices of bacon. Make sure the bacon completely covers the avocado.

5 Brown the bacon on all sides in a frying pan coated lightly with oil.

You'll need

- 1 avocado
- 1 egg
- 5 slices of bacon

Preparation Time: 20 min
Cooking Time: 10 min
Servings: 1

tip

Sprinkle a dash of paprika on the egg before putting it in the avocado.

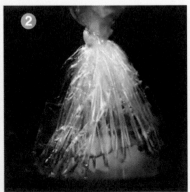

Bacon Avocado Surprise

Here's how:

1. Spread the pizza dough onto a work surface and coat the dough with a generous portion of pizza sauce.

2. Add some oregano followed by grated mozzarella and pepperoni slices. Be sure to leave some space along the edges so the ingredients don't fall out during the next step.

3. Tightly roll up the pizza dough and cut it into 1-inch pieces.

4. Put the pieces on a baking tray and bake for 12 minutes at 390°F.

5. After baking, finish off your lollipops with a decorative straw or popsicle stick.

You'll need

- 1 package pizza dough
- pizza sauce
- pepperoni
- grated mozzarella cheese
- oregano

🕐 Preparation Time: 10 min
Cooking Time: 12 min

👥 Servings: 15

tip

Make a Hawaiian version with some finely chopped ham and pineapple.

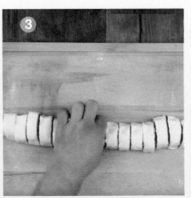

Pizza Lollipops

Here's how:

1. Remove the crusts from the bread slices and roll them out with a rolling pin.

2. Place the rolled out slices on a baking sheet.

3. Add the crème fraîche, prosciutto, diced onion and cheese to a mixing bowl and mix them thoroughly. If the mix is too thick, add a splash of cream to it.

4. Spread the cheese mixture onto the slices of bread and bake at 390°F for 15 minutes.

You'll need

- 4 slices of white bread
- prosciutto, chopped
- ¾ cup crème fraîche
- ½ an onion, diced
- 1½ cups grated cheese

🕐 Preparation Time: 10 min
Cooking Time: 15 min

👥 Servings: 4

tip

To make your flambé extra savory sprinkle on some chopped chives.

34

Toast Flambé

Here's how:

1 To prepare the meatballs, combine the ground beef and onion, season with salt and pepper, and roll the meat into golfball-sized balls. Coat a frying pan with a little oil and brown the meatballs on all sides.

2 Mix the cooked spaghetti with 3.5 oz parmesan (save a little for garnishing) and a few drops of olive oil.

3 Swirl the spaghetti onto a fork against a spoon until you have a good-sized portion. Gently press it into a muffin mold.

4 Add a spoonful of tomato sauce to the middle of the noodle basket, place a meatball on top, follow with another dollop of sauce and sprinkle with parmesan.

5 Bake at 375°F for 20 minutes.

You'll need

- 5 oz ground beef
- 1 onion, finely chopped
- 3.5 oz cooked spaghetti
- 4 oz grated parmesan cheese
- 4 oz tomato sauce

Preparation Time: 15 min
Cooking Time: 20 min

Servings: 6

tip

Garnish your baskets with some fresh finely-chopped basil.

36

Spaghetti & Meatball Baskets

Meals & More

Here's how:

1. Grate the parmesan cheese and place it in a round, flat circle on a baking tray covered with parchment paper. Bake for 6 to 7 minutes at 370°F.

2. After baking, remove the cheese from the parchment paper with a spatula and place it over the outside of a bowl. The bottom of the bowl should be facing down. As the cheese cools it will remain in this bowl shape.

3. While the cheese is cooling, cook the spaghetti al dente and save about a ½ cup of pasta water.

4. Add the cooked spaghetti, olive oil, and the rest of the parmesan cheese to this water and mix it all together until the spaghetti is swimming in a creamy sauce.

5. Let the pasta cool and serve it in the cheese bowl with some extra parmesan sprinkled on top.

You'll need

- 6 oz parmesan cheese
- 3.5 oz spaghetti
- 3 tbsp olive oil

🕐 Preparation Time: 15 min
Cooking Time: 6-7 min

👥 Servings: 1

tip ————

Sprinkle on some fresh herbs before serving.

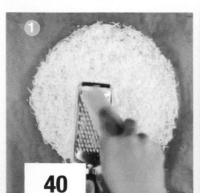

40

Parmesan Pasta Bowl

Here's how:

1. Shuck and core the pineapple. Keep the bottom and top so you can use them later.

2. Cut the chicken breast into three equal strips and marinate them in a mixture of oil, cayenne pepper, salt and pepper.

3. Stuff the marinated chicken strips into the hollowed out pineapple and then season the outside with cayenne pepper.

4. Wrap the seasoned pineapple in bacon slices using toothpicks to hold them in place if necessary.

5. Coat the bacon slices with barbecue sauce.

6. Put the top and bottom back on the pineapple and secure them with skewers.

7. Grill your "swineapple" for 45-60 minutes.

You'll need

- 1 pineapple
- 7 oz chicken breast
- 10 oz bacon
- 3 tbsp cayenne pepper
- 2 tbsp barbecue sauce

🕐 Preparation Time: 15 min
Cooking Time: 45-60 min

👥 Servings: 4

 tip

Add some paprika to the marinade and the outside of the pineapple to give it some extra zing.

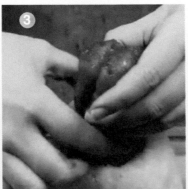

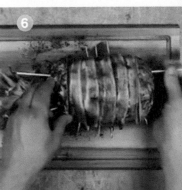

BBQ Swineapple

Here's how:

1. Spread out the pizza dough and use a small springform pan to cut three circular portions. Bake these for 10 minutes at 355°F.

2. Form a ball with the remaining dough and then roll it out on a floured surface making sure that it is longer than it is wide. Use it to line the sides of the springform pan.

3. Press one of the baked portions of dough onto the bottom of the springform pan.

4. Now cover it with pizza sauce, some cheese, and some pepperoni before placing the next dough portion on top. Repeat this process to create two more layers.

5. When the layers are done, you can tuck in the edges of the dough lining on the sides to give your layer cake pizza a more finished look.

6. Bake for 40 minutes at 355°F.

You'll need

- pizza dough
- flour
- 2 cups pizza sauce
- 4 cups grated cheese
- 7 oz pepperoni or salami

🕐 Preparation Time: 20 min
Cooking Time: 40 min
🧑‍🤝‍🧑 Servings: 4

tip

Use ham and pineapple instead of pepperoni to make a Hawaiian Layer Cake Pizza.

44

Layer Cake Pizza

Here's how:

1. Mix the paprika, curry powder, chili powder and olive oil to make the marinade.

2. Cut the tenderloin lengthwise into three equal-sized pieces, but don't cut right to the end.

3. Now braid the three pieces and baste the tenderloin with marinade.

4. Put the marinated tenderloin on an oven tray and bake for 30 minutes at 375°F.

You'll need

- 1 pork tenderloin
- 1 tbsp paprika
- 1 tsp curry powder
- 1 tsp chili powder
- 3 tbsp olive oil

🕐 Preparation Time: 20 min
Cooking Time: 30 min

👥 Servings: 3-4

tip

Put some potatoes coated with olive oil and chopped rosemary in the oven at the same time to make a tasty side dish.

46

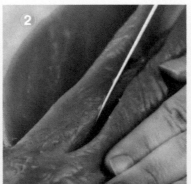

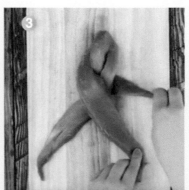

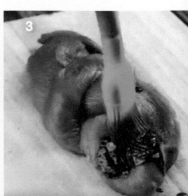

Marinated Tenderloin Twist

Here's how:

1. Use a peeler to cut the zucchini into thin strips.

2. Do the same with the bell pepper.

3. Put the vegetables in a baking dish, add the rest of the ingredients, season with salt and pepper and mix well.

4. Bake for 8-9 minutes at 400°F.

You'll need

- 2 zucchinis
- 1 yellow bell pepper
- 6-9 shrimp
- 1 clove of garlic, chopped
- 1 tbsp olive oil

🕐 Preparation Time: 10 min
Cooking Time: 8-9 min

👥 Servings: 2

tip ———

Squeeze some lemon juice on after baking to make it extra zesty.

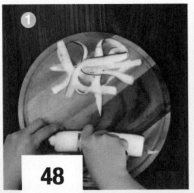

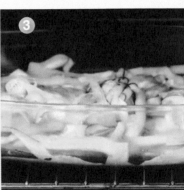

Zucchini Pasta with Shrimp

Here's how:

1. Slice the baguette lengthwise but take care not to cut it all the way through. The two halves should still be connected.

2. Fill the baguette with layers of grated mozzarella, salami and cheese slices.

3. Close the baguette and press it firmly together.

4. Place the strips of bacon lengthwise overlapping each other on a flat surface and put the baguette on top of them. Wrap the bacon around the entire baguette.

5. Bake the whole thing in a preheated oven for 45 minutes at 340°F.

You'll need

- 1 large baguette
- 12 oz salami
- 12 oz bacon
- 7 oz cheese slices
- 5 oz grated mozzarella

 Preparation Time: 25 min
Cooking Time: 45 min
Servings: 6-8

tip ———
Add a layer of your favorite sandwich sauce or have some ready for dipping when it's done.

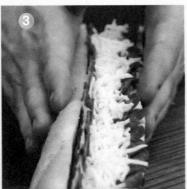

Bacon-Wrapped Salami Baguette

Here's how:

1. Grate the potatoes and mix them with 1 cup of cheese and 2 eggs. Season with salt and pepper.

2. Spoon the hash brown mix onto a baking tray and form it into a circle.

3. Bake at 400°F for 12 minutes.

4. While the hash brown mix is baking, fry up the bacon slices and cut them into small pieces.

5. Sprinkle the rest of the cheese on the baked hash browns. Form a circle along the edge of the hash browns using the bacon cubes before making two lines that cross each other at the center of the hash browns.

6. Break an egg into each quarter of the hash browns.

7. Bake the dish for another 15 minutes at 400°F.

You'll need

- 10 oz peeled potatoes
- 1 cup grated cheddar cheese
- 6 eggs
- 6 slices of bacon

🕐 Preparation Time: 15 min
Cooking Time: 27 min

👥 Servings: 2-4

tip ———

Make your meal extra savory with a sprinkle of freshly chopped chives.

Bacon & Egg
Hash Browns

Here's how:

1. Mix the ricotta cheese, cream and dill in a bowl.

2. Roll out the pizza dough and put it on a lined baking tray. Spread the dill cream evenly over the dough.

3. Cut the smoked salmon into small pieces and distribute it evenly over the dill cream.

4. Roll up the dough and cut it lengthwise to form two long pieces.

5. Twist the pieces into a braid and connect the ends.

6. Bake for 30 minutes at 350°F.

You'll need

- 4-5 oz smoked salmon
- ⅔ cup ricotta cheese
- 1 sheet pizza dough
- ¼ cup cream
- 1 tbsp dill

🕐 Preparation Time: 15 min
Cooking Time: 30 min

👥 Servings: 1

tip

Add a squeeze of fresh lemon juice before eating.

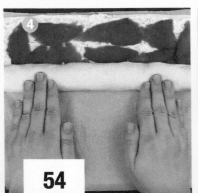

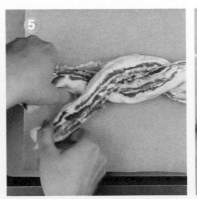
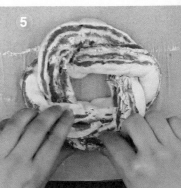

Braided Salmon Roll

Here's how:

① Place the bacon slices in a pie pan or skillet so that they overlap and form a circle. The ends of the slices should hang well over the edge of the pan. The surface of the pan should be completely covered.

② Wash the potatoes and cut them into thin slices.

③ Place a layer of potato slices on the bacon, season with salt and pepper, and cover with grated cheese. Repeat this two more times, each time adding fewer potato slices.

④ Fold the ends of the bacon slices over to cover the final layer of cheese.

⑤ Bake for 2.5 hours at 340°F.

You'll need

- 45 slices of bacon
- 5 medium-sized potatoes
- 14 oz cheddar cheese

🕐 Preparation Time: 25 min
Cooking Time: 2.5 hrs

👥 Servings: 6-8

tip

Have a little ketchup or barbecue sauce ready on your plate for dipping.

Bacon & Potato Pie

Here's how:

1. Spread out the puff pastry dough and place the hot dogs in the center with four lined up next to each other and another row of four behind them.

2. Lay the cheese slices on top.

3. Add a layer of sliced pickles.

4. Cut the extra puff pastry on both sides into equal-sized slanted strips of dough.

5. Fold the strips of dough over the filling alternating from both sides. This creates the woven appearance. Make sure to press the ends.

6. Coat the top of the pastry with beaten egg.

7. Bake for 20 minutes at 375°F.

You'll need

- 1 sheet puff pastry dough
- 8 hot dogs
- 3 slices of cheese
- pickles
- 1 egg, beaten

🕐 Preparation Time: 25 min
   Cooking Time: 20 min

👥 Servings: 4-6

tip ———

Add some extra flavor with a layer of roasted onions and make sure to have some mustard and ketchup ready for dipping.

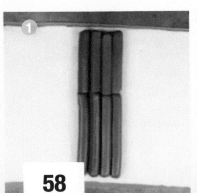

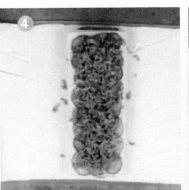

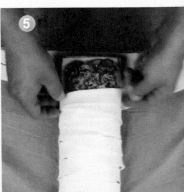

Hot Dog Pastry Braid

Here's how:

① Cut 14 oz of zucchini into slices and brown them in a grill pan on both sides.

② Season the cooked rice with salt and pepper and mix in the eggs and parmesan.

③ Line the bottom and sides of a bundt-bottom springform pan with the grilled zucchini slices so that they overlap and form a seamless hull for the other ingredients. Leave an inch or two of the slice hanging over the edge of the pan.

④ Add half the rice to the pan and press an indention in the center of it all the way around. Fill it with 3 oz of diced zucchini and ham.

⑤ Cover with the other half of the rice and press it firmly into the form. Fold the overlapping zucchini slices back over the rice.

⑥ Bake at 350°F for 25 minutes.

You'll need

- 17 oz zucchini
- 2 cups cooked rice
- 3 eggs
- 1 cup grated parmesan cheese
- 5 oz ham, diced

🕐 Preparation Time: 25 min
Cooking Time: 25 min

👥 Servings: 4-6

tip

Add some mozzarella to the filling to make it extra cheesy.

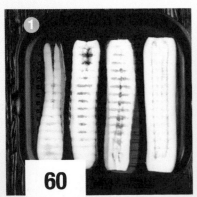

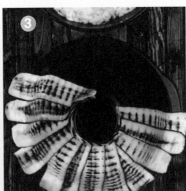

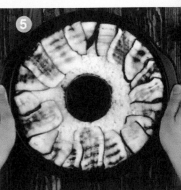

Zucchini Rice Ring

Here's how:

1. Wash the potatoes and cut them into very thin slices. The peel can be left on if you prefer.

2. Add a layer of potato slices to the bottom of a large casserole dish.

3. Pour the bolognese sauce onto the potato layer.

4. Now add the baby spinach and a layer of cheese.

5. Keep adding layers until the casserole dish is full. The final layer should be cheese.

6. Bake for 1.5 hours at 320°F.

You'll need

- 3 large waxy potatoes
- 2¼ cups bolognese sauce
- 2 oz baby spinach
- 10 oz grated mozzarella cheese

 Preparation Time: 20 min
Cooking Time: 1.5 hrs

Servings: 4-6

tip ———

Experiment with different cheeses to make your own unique creation.

Potato Lasagna

Here's how:

1. Cut one potato lengthwise into thin slices and the other one crosswise into thin slices.

2. Heat a little oil in a frying pan and brown the potato slices on both sides.

3. Cover the bottom of a springform pan with the smaller potato slices and use the longer slices to line the sides.

4. Mix the remaining ingredients in a bowl until you achieve a consistent mixture.

5. Pour the mixture onto the potatoes and spread it out evenly.

6. Bake for 30 minutes at 320°F.

You'll need

- 2 large potatoes
- 12 oz spinach
- 8 oz cream cheese
- 1.3 oz feta cheese
- 2 eggs

🕐 Preparation Time: 25 min
Cooking Time: 30 min

👥 Servings: 6-8

tip ———

Make your pie extra savory by adding some finely chopped onion to the mix.

Spinach &
Potato Pie

Here's how:

1. Slice the top off the loaf of bread to serve as a lid.

2. Place the wheel of camembert in the center and trace around it with a knife. Pull out the bread inside this circle until it is deep enough for the cheese wheel to fit inside.

3. Peel and boil the potatoes. As soon as they are cooked, wrap each potato in a half slice of bacon.

4. Cover the cheese wheel and bread bowl with its lid and wrap it in aluminum foil.

5. Bake the bread and the bacon-wrapped potatoes on separate baking sheets for 30 minutes at 355°F.

You'll need

- 1 round rustic loaf
- 1 whole camembert
- 16 small potatoes
- 8 slices bacon

🕐 Preparation Time: 15 min
Cooking Time: 30 min

👥 Servings: 4

tip ——

Add some more flavor by sprinkling chopped spring onions onto the melted cheese.

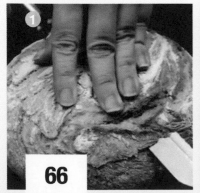

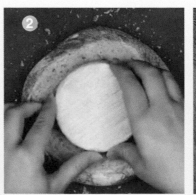

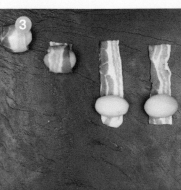

Cheese Fondue with Bacon Wrapped Potatoes

Here's how:

① Heat some oil in a pan and sauté the spinach until it's soft.

② Add the sour cream and stir. Season with salt and pepper.

③ Squeeze some lemon juice into the sauce and let it continue to simmer.

④ Add the cooked pasta and salmon cubes to the mix and cook for another 2-3 minutes.

⑤ Stir and serve.

You'll need

- 10.5 oz wild salmon, cubed
- 7 oz spinach
- 1¼ cups sour cream
- 3 tbsp lemon juice
- 8 oz cooked pasta

🕐 Preparation Time: 10 min
Cooking Time: 15 min
👥 Servings: 3-4

tip ——————

Sprinkle on some parmesan cheese for the crowning touch.

Spinach &
Salmon Pasta

Here's how:

1. Pour the milk into a pan and stir in the cream cheese while keeping it at a low heat.

2. Add the chopped garlic and about 5 oz of grated cheddar. Stir until the cheese is completely melted.

3. Chop up the boiled cauliflower and put it in a casserole dish.

4. Pour the cheesy sauce on top and season with salt and pepper.

5. Sprinkle the rest of the cheddar on top.

6. Bake at 320°F for 40 minutes.

You'll need

- 2 heads of cauliflower, boiled
- 3 cloves of garlic, chopped
- 1¾ cups milk
- 7 oz grated cheddar cheese
- 3.5 oz cream cheese

🕐 Preparation Time: 25 min
Cooking Time: 40 min

👥 Servings: 6-8

tip ————

Add some spring onions and bacon to make it even heartier.

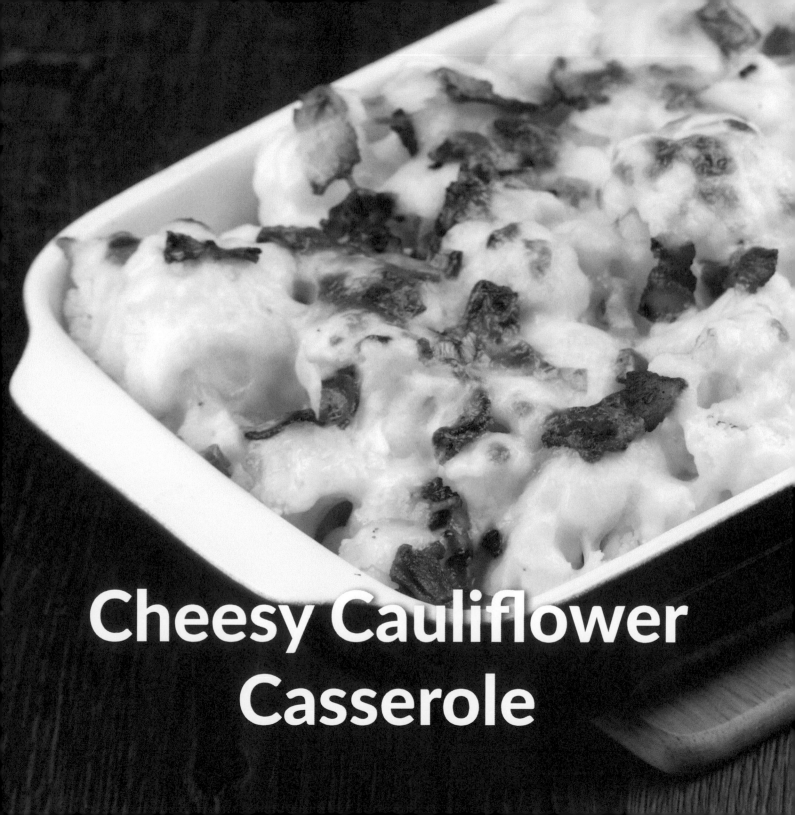

Cheesy Cauliflower Casserole

Here's how:

1. Roll out the pastry dough on a baking tray lined with parchment paper. Cut it into triangles and arrange them in a star shape with the tips pointing out.

2. Place a slice of bacon on each point of the star.

3. Arrange a ring of grated cheese on top of the bacon at the center of the star.

4. Scramble 5 eggs with salt, pepper, and diced bell pepper.

5. Spoon the scrambled eggs onto the grated cheddar in the center of the dough.

6. Add a second layer of grated cheddar cheese on top of the eggs.

7. Now take the outer tips of the pastry dough and fold them into the center creating a ring.

8. Brush with beaten egg and bake at 350°F for 20 minutes.

You'll need

- 1 sheet of crescent dough
- 8 slices of bacon
- 6 eggs
- ½ bell pepper, diced
- grated cheddar cheese

🕐 Preparation Time: 20 min
Cooking Time: 20 min

👥 Servings: 2-4

tip ———

Experiment with different cheese to create your own unique version.

Bacon & Egg Breakfast Turnover

Here's how:

1 Pour the milk into a pan, add the macaroni, season with salt and pepper, then bring it to a boil. Make sure to stir frequently to keep the milk from burning.

2 Add 1⅔ cups of cheese and the tomatoes. Mix until the cheese has melted.

3 If you're not using a cast iron pan, put the mix in a casserole dish so it's ready for the oven.

4 Sprinkle the rest of the cheese and the breadcrumbs over the top.

5 Bake for 10 minutes at 350°F.

You'll need

- 1¼ cups milk
- 3.5 oz giant macaroni
- 2 cups grated cheddar cheese
- ⅓ cup diced tomatoes
- ⅓ cup breadcrumbs

🕐 Preparation Time: 15 min
Cooking Time: 10 min

👥 Servings: 3

tip ———

Add some crumbled potato chips to the breadcrumbs for extra flavor.

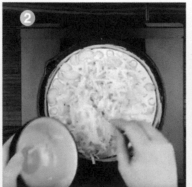

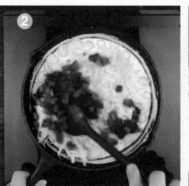

Baked
Mac & Cheese

Here's how:

1. Cut and then replace the top of the camembert, placing it in the center of a springform pan.

2. Cook the spaghetti al dente in salt water and drain.

3. Cut the bacon into short strips and brown it in a pan.

4. Mix the pasta, bacon, parmesan, and eggs in a large mixing bowl until the pasta is well coated.

5. Arrange the pasta around the camembert and bake at 410°F for 15 minutes.

You'll need

- 9 oz spaghetti, uncooked
- 7 oz bacon
- 4 eggs
- 1 cup grated parmesan cheese
- 1 whole camembert

🕐 Preparation Time: 15 min
Cooking Time: 15 min

👥 Servings: 4-6

tip ————

Adorn your crown with a garnish of fresh basil leaves and cherry tomatoes.

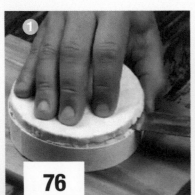

Carbonara Camembert Crown

Here's how:

1. Wash the peppers and cut them into thick strips. Cut the puff pastry into two pieces, one measuring 6 x 8 inches and the other around 7.5 x 8 inches. Take the smaller of the pieces and cut it into 17 strips.

2. Place 13 strips right next to each other. At the end, place another strip on top of the 13 strips, but in the opposite direction. Pull every second strip over the end as if turning a page of a book.

3. Place a row of red peppers on top of the strips that are not pulled over before pulling the original strips back over to cover the pepper. Repeat this weaving process with alternating colors.

4. When you reach the end, place another strip to close off the pattern. The two extra strips of dough should be placed at the top and the bottom so that the colorful masterpiece is properly framed.

5. Brush the larger piece of pastry with egg and then place the ham in the middle, followed by the mozzarella. Season with salt and pepper.

6. Place the colorful braided pastry on top of the ham and cheese. To close the pie, fold the edges of the larger bottom pastry over the edges of the top.

7. Brush the entire pie with beaten egg and bake for 25 minutes at 375°F.

You'll need

- 4 peppers (green, red, yellow, orange)
- 1 sheet puff pastry dough
- 4 slices of ham
- 4.5 oz mozzarella
- 1 egg

🕐 Preparation Time: 20 min
Cooking Time: 25 min

👥 Servings: 3-4

tip ———
Add some diced onion to make it extra savory.

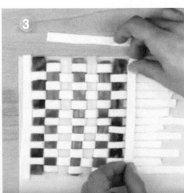

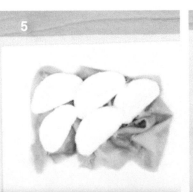

Ham & Pepper Pie

Sweets
&
Treats

Here's how:

1. Preheat your oven to 375°F. Roll out the first sheet of puff pastry dough onto a baking tray lined with parchment paper.

2. Spoon the chocolate spread onto the middle of the dough sheet and spread it into the shape of a triangle with the back of a spoon.

3. Cover it with the second sheet of pastry dough and use a knife to cut out the triangle.

4. Cut two 1-inch wide strips at the bottom of the tree, leaving a strip in the center as the tree trunk.

5. Use this trunk as a guide and cut lines from the center to the left and right, about an inch apart at the bottom and gradually closer together near the top.

6. Twist each strip at the bottom twice so that it forms a loose spiral.

7. For the shorter strips at the top, a single twist is enough.

8. Cut a star shape from the remaining dough and add it to the tip of the Christmas tree.

9. Brush the entire tree with beaten egg and put it in the oven.

10. Bake at 375°F for 15 minutes.

You'll need

- 2 rolls puff pastry dough
- 4 tbsp chocolate spread (or Nutella)
- 1 egg, beaten

Preparation Time: 15 min
Cooking Time: 15 min

Servings: 4-6

tip

Decorate your tree with some sprinkles and crushed nuts.

82

Chocolate Christmas Tree

Here's how:

① Cut the bananas into pieces.

② Put the banana pieces in a freezer-safe container and freeze them for at least 2 hours.

③ Now purée the frozen bananas in a blender until smooth.

④ Scoop and enjoy!

You'll need

- 3 ripe bananas

🕐 Preparation Time: 10 min

👥 Servings: 1

tip ────

Add an extra flavor dimension with a sprinkle of cinnamon.

84

Banana Ice Treat

Here's how:

1 Mix the sugar and cinnamon together and spread about half of it on a large working surface.

2 Roll out the puff pastry dough on the working surface and sprinkle the rest of the sugar and cinnamon mix on top.

3 Roll a rolling pin across the dough so that the sugar and cinnamon mix is pressed in underneath and on top.

4 On each long side of the dough fold half an inch over toward the middle and press the fold down well so it doesn't unfold again.

5 Starting with one of the half-inch folds, roll the whole side up carefully all the way to the middle. Do the same on the other side.

6 The dough should now be two equal-sized rolls joined at the bottom. Cut it in 1-inch slices across and lay each slice onto a baking sheet on its back. The cookies will expand so leave enough room between them on the sheet.

7 Bake for 8 min at 480°F.

You'll need

- 1 roll puff pastry dough
- ⅔ cup sugar
- 2 tsp cinnamon

🕐 Preparation Time: 15 min
Cooking Time: 8 min

👥 Servings: 6-8

tip ————
Have a glass of milk ready for dunking.

86

Cinnamon Palmier Cookies

Here's how:

① Remove the crust from the bread slices and roll them flat with a rolling pin.

② Scoop out a single scoop of ice cream and freeze it until it is well-hardened.

③ Place the hardened scoop of ice cream on a slice of flattened bread and lay the other slice on top. Now wrap the bread around the ice cream. Freeze the ice cream wrapped in bread until it is hard before continuing with the next step.

④ Prepare some hot oil and deep fry the bread-covered ice cream for 15 seconds. Mix the cinnamon and sugar and roll your breaded ice cream in the mix.

⑤ Top off your hot vanilla delight with some chocolate sauce and enjoy!

You'll need

- 1 scoop vanilla ice cream
- 2 slices of brown bread
- 1 tbsp cinnamon
- ½ cup sugar
- chocolate sauce

🕐 Preparation Time: 20 min

👥 Servings: 1

tip ———

Sprinkle on some crushed almonds for the crowning touch.

88

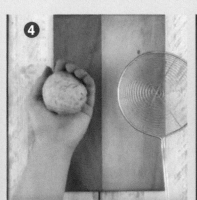

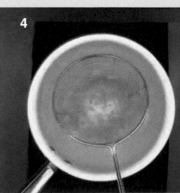

Hot Vanilla Delight

Here's how:

1 Dunk the Ladyfingers in a ½ cup of milk for a short time, place them on plastic wrap and refrigerate for 4 hours.

2 Heat 2 cups of milk, add the pudding mix, and cook the pudding according to the instructions

3 When the pudding has cooled, spread it onto the Ladyfingers.

4 Peel the banana and place it over the bottom third of the the Ladyfingers.

5 Roll the whole thing up carefully in the plastic wrap and refrigerate for one more hour.

6 Remove the roll from the plastic wrap and decorate it with whipped cream.

You'll need

- 12 Ladyfingers
- 2½ cups milk
- 1 package vanilla pudding mix
- 1 banana
- whipped cream

🕐 Preparation Time: 15 min

👥 Servings: 3

tip

Sprinkle on some cocoa powder or use chocolate pudding instead of vanilla pudding to make a chocolatey version.

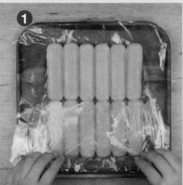

Ladyfinger Roll

Here's how:

1 Put all of the ingredients into a bowl and mix well.

2 Pour the mixture into a greased baking pan and spread evenly.

3 Bake for 15 minutes at 350°F.

You'll need

- 1 large jar of chocolate spread (or Nutella) (approx. 26 oz)
- 4 eggs
- 1¼ cups flour

🕑 Preparation Time: 10 min
Cooking Time: 15 min
👥 Servings: 12

tip

Sprinkle on some powdered sugar after baking for an extra sweet kick.

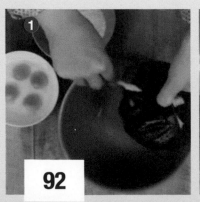

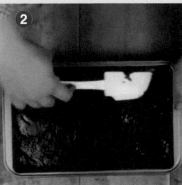

Super Fast Brownies

Here's how:

1 Peel, core, and cut both apples into small cubes.

2 Put the apples, sugar, cinnamon and about a ½ cup of water into a pot. Cover and bring to a boil. Once the apples are soft, use a hand mixer to blend them to a sauce.

3 Roll the pastry dough onto a baking tray lined with parchment paper and cut it in the middle.

4 Spread the apple mixture on one half of the pastry and then place the other half on top.

5 Using a pizza cutter, cut the apple-filled pastry into equal-sized fingers.

6 Brush with beaten egg and sprinkle on some cinnamon and sugar.

7 Bake for 10-14 minutes at 350°F.

You'll need

- 2 apples
- ⅓ cup sugar
- 2 tbsp cinnamon
- 1 sheet puff pastry dough
- 1 egg, beaten

🕐 Preparation Time: 30 min
Cooking Time: 10-14 min

👥 Servings: 2-3

tip ——————

Have some vanilla sauce or hot caramel ready for dipping.

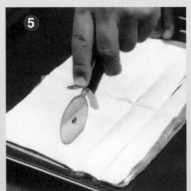

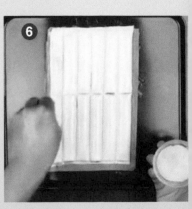

Cinnamon Apple Fingers

Here's how:

1. Cut the white chocolate into small pieces and melt it in a bowl suspended over boiling water.

2. After the chocolate is melted, pour it into three silicone cupcake liners and then pour it out immediately leaving the forms lined (not filled) with white chocolate. Let the chocolate harden. Placing it in the refrigerator can speed up this process.

3. Remove the chocolate cups, dip the rims into the melted chocolate and then into the rainbow sprinkles.

4. Add the remaining chocolate to a piping bag. Squeeze out three large circles and three "C" shapes onto a piece of parchment paper.

5. When these have hardened, pipe a couple of drops of melted chocolate into the middle of the circle and stick the chocolate cup into it.

6. Dip the ends of the handle in melted chocolate and press it onto the side of the cup, if necessary holding it there until the chocolate starts to harden.

7. Melt the dark chocolate and stir in the whipped cream.

8. Pipe the chocolate mousse into the chocolate cups and garnish with a maraschino cherry.

You'll need

- 14 oz white chocolate
- 3.5 oz dark chocolate
- 2½ cups whipped cream
- rainbow sprinkles
- 3 maraschino cherries

🕐 Preparation Time: 15 min

👥 Servings: 3

tip

Try out different toppings to match the occasion, e.g. chocolate hearts for Valentine's Day.

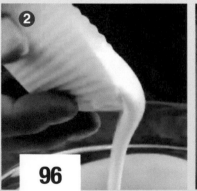

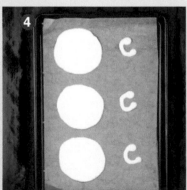

Chocolate Teacups

Here's how:

① Cut off the top of the apples and use a spoon to hollow them out without damaging the outer shell. Keep the apple bits you scoop out.

② Mix the bits of apple with the pecans, brown sugar and some butter.

③ Fill the hollowed apples with the mixture.

④ Using the "lid" of the apple that you cut off, trace and cut out two circles of dough from the shortcrust pastry sheet.

⑤ Cut thin strips out of the remaining dough and weave them overtop the stuffed apples. Now set both apples on top of the two dough circles in a baking pan.

⑥ Coat the weaved dough with beaten egg and sprinkle more brown sugar on top.

⑦ Bake for 30 minutes at 340°F.

You'll need

- 2 apples
- 1 oz pecans
- 1.5 oz brown sugar
- 1 egg
- 1 sheet puff pastry dough

🕐 Preparation Time: 20 min
Cooking Time: 30 min

👥 Servings: 2

tip —————

Make your apples extra tasty with a scoop of vanilla ice cream and some caramel sauce.

Baked Apple Dream

Here's how:

1. Melt the semisweet chocolate in a bowl suspended over boiling water.

2. Put a spoonful of melted chocolate in the middle of a dessert plate and let it start to harden. Prepare four of these plates.

3. Blow up four small balloons (approx. 3 inches across) and wipe them clean. Make sure they are completely dry.

4. Dip them into the rest of the melted chocolate.

5. Press each chocolate-coated balloon into a circle of chocolate on a dessert plate. Hold it until the chocolate hardens so it stays in place.

6. When the chocolate is completely hard, you can carefully pop the balloons and remove them.

7. For the mousse filling, melt the white chocolate and mix it with the whipped cream.

8. Pipe the mixture into the egg-shells.

9. Hollow out a little spot in the middle of the mousse and add a dollop of jam to make the "yolk."

You'll need

- 14 oz semisweet chocolate
- 3.5 white chocolate
- 2 cups whipped cream
- 4 tbsp jam, apricot or peach
- 4 balloons

🕐 Preparation Time: 35 min

👥 Servings: 4

tip —————
Add some fun color to your egg with a dash of candy sprinkles.

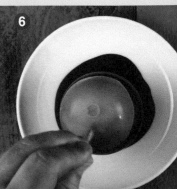

Chocolate Cream Egg

Here's how:

① Cut the lemons lengthwise and use a spoon to hollow out the halves keeping the lemon rinds intact. Put your lemon pulp in a sieve and press the juice into a bowl.

② Put the sugar, blackberries and lemon juice into a pot. Once boiling, reduce heat and let simmer for 5 minutes.

③ Remove the pot from the stove and use the back of a spoon to press the mixture through a sieve and into a bowl.

④ When the mixture is lukewarm, stir in the butter. Once cooled, take a small amount from the bowl and use the back of a spoon to lightly coat the lemon rind bowls with the blackberry mixture.

⑤ Now mix the whipped cream into the blackberry mixture.

⑥ Gently spoon the mixture into the lemon bowls and let freeze for 12 hours.

You'll need

- 4 large lemons
- 3.5 oz blackberries (fresh or frozen)
- ½ cup sugar
- ½ cup whipped cream
- 1 tbsp butter

🕐 Preparation Time: 20 min

👥 Servings: 8

tip

This technique works just as well with other fruits, e.g. raspberry ice cream in an orange bowl.

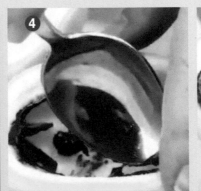

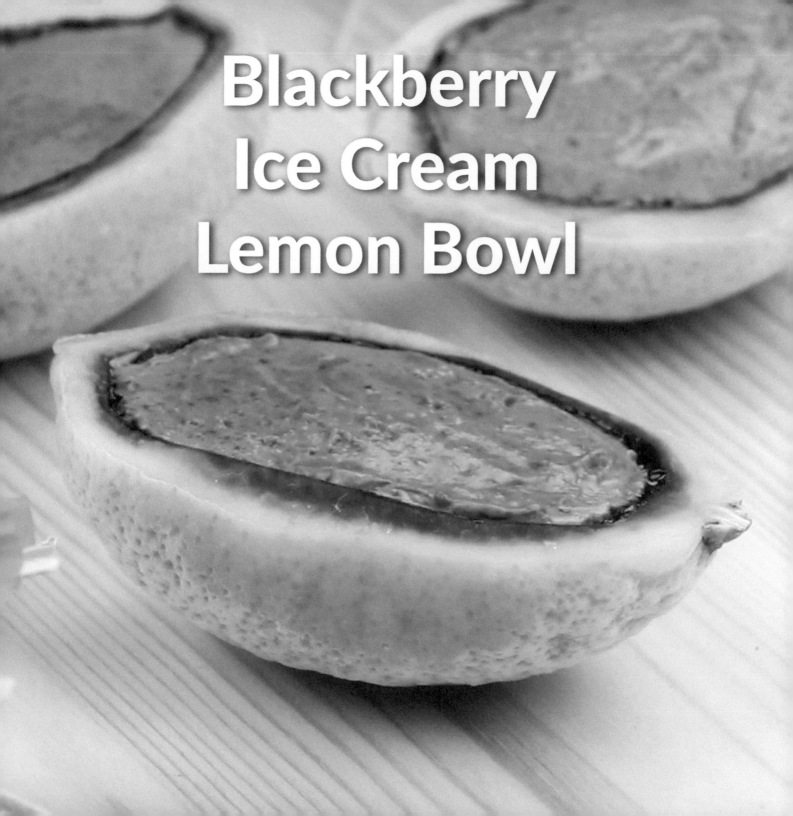

Blackberry
Ice Cream
Lemon Bowl

Here's how:

1 Cut up the chocolate and melt it in a bowl suspended over boiling water.

2 Mix the butter into the melted chocolate.

3 In a second bowl, beat the eggs and sugar until frothy.

4 Add the flour to the beaten egg and mix until smooth.

5 Pour in the melted chocolate and butter and mix well.

6 Pour the mix evenly into the six molds of a muffin pan.

7 Bake for 7 minutes at 430°F.

You'll need

- 4 oz butter
- 3 oz dark chocolate
- ½ cup sugar
- ⅓ cup flour
- 4 eggs

🕐 Preparation Time: 20 min
Cooking Time: 7 min

👥 Servings: 6

tip

Sprinkle on some powdered sugar before serving.

Molten Chocolate Cupcakes

Here's how:

1 Cut the banana into 12 thick slices. Place them on one side of the rolled out pastry dough.

2 Cut the dough into 12 strips that are exactly as wide as the banana slices.

3 Warm up the chocolate spread in the microwave and pour it over the banana slices.

4 Roll up the dough starting on the side with the banana slices.

5 Lay the roll on a baking tray around a small ovenproof bowl to form a ring.

6 Baste the dough with beaten egg and put chunks of chocolate in the bowl.

7 Bake at 360°F for 20 minutes.

You'll need

- 2 bananas
- 1 sheet of puff pastry
- 4.5 oz chocolate spread (or Nutella)
- 5 oz chocolate
- 1 egg, beaten

Preparation Time: 20 min
Cooking Time: 20 min

Servings: 3-4

tip

Use peanut butter instead of chocolate spread and enjoy a new flavor dimension.

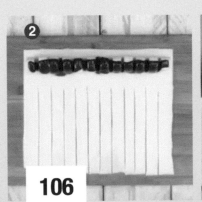

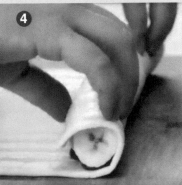

106

Chocolate Banana Ring

Here's how:

① Cut the chocolate into small pieces and melt them in a bowl suspended over boiling water.

② Add the butter and cream and mix thoroughly.

③ Place a layer of Oreo cookies in the bottom of a loaf pan.

④ Pour the melted chocolate over the cookie layer so it is completely covered.

⑤ Add another layer of Oreo cookies and cover it with chocolate. Repeat this process until the pan is full.

⑥ Refrigerate the cake for 8 hours.

You'll need

- 28 oz bittersweet chocolate
- 7 oz butter
- 1 cup cream
- 40 Oreo cookies

🕐 Preparation Time: 15 min

👥 Servings: 4-6

tip

Experiment with different kinds of cookies to make your own unique creation.

Oreo
Cold Cake

Here's how:

① Line a springform pan with parchment paper making sure to cover the sides and rim.

② Mix the raspberries with about 3 oz of powdered sugar and mash them up with a fork.

③ Mix the mascarpone with 3.5 oz of powdered sugar and a pinch of salt.

④ Cut 12 Ladyfingers in half and lay them in the springform pan to form the bottom layer of the cake.

⑤ Spread half the raspberry mixture on top of the Ladyfinger layer and press it down firmly with a spoon.

⑥ Spread on half the mascarpone mix to make the next layer.

⑦ Cut the other 12 Ladyfingers in half and use them to make the next cake layer.

⑧ Spread the rest of the raspberry mixture on the Ladyfingers followed by another layer of mascarpone.

⑨ Top it off with a layer of blueberries.

You'll need

- 24 Ladyfingers
- 23 oz mascarpone
- 6.5 oz powdered sugar
- 9 oz blueberries
- 21 oz raspberries

🕐 Preparation Time: 25 min

👥 Servings: 6-8

tip ————

Dash on some powdered sugar to give your cake an extra sweet kick.

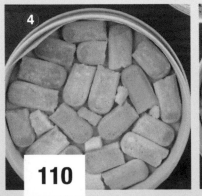

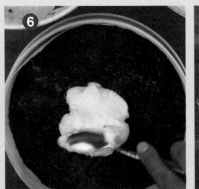

Ladyfinger Berry Cake

Starters & Snacks

Meals & More

Sweets & Treats

The Scrumdiddlyumptious Team:
they make it possible...

Production Management
Inken Dworak
Joana Cidade
Marco Ogrzewalla
Patrick Piel

Videography & Photography
Joscha Durand
Giacomo Merchich
Oliver Fröhlich
Quan Tran
Niklas Thelen
Oliver Taranczewski
Lara Nelles
Ju Yong Kim

Production Assistants
Sarah Heitzler
Isabell Griesert

Chefs
Gregor Brühs
Oliver Stilla
Cristina Renz
Hannes Tschoep

Book Design
Nicolas Buenaventura Arango

Book Layout
Nicolas Buenaventura Arango
James Qureitem
Kosuke Nishimoto

Book Text & Editing
Paul McCormick
Stephanie Körhle
James Qureitem

www.scrumdiddlyumptious.com

f facebook.com/scrumdiddlyumptiouscom

▶ youtube.com/scrumdiddlyumptious

ISBN: 978-3-00-057781-9

Printed in Great Britain
by Amazon